101 Amazin
Do in l

Introduction

So you're going to Mexico, huh? You are very lucky indeed! You are sure in for a treat because Mexico is truly one of the most magical countries in the world. There's a mix of incredible ancient ruins, awesome restaurants and street food, and outdoor adventure activities and shopping that makes Mexico one of the most enduringly popular tourist destinations on the face of the earth.

In this guide, we'll be giving you the low down on:
- the very best things to shove in your pie hole, from street food staples like tacos al pastor to restaurants that are over 100 years old
- the best shopping so that you can take a little piece of Mexico back home with you, whether that's in the form of a hand crafted rug or a bottle of mezcal
- incredible festivals, whether you want to the experiment of mariachi bands or you want to party on the beach at a bangin' dance festival
- the coolest historical and cultural sights that you simply cannot afford to miss like Frida Kahlo's House and the largest pyramid in the world

- where to party like someone from Mexico and get down with the locals
- and tonnes more coolness besides!

Let's not waste any more time – here are the 101 most amazing, spectacular, and coolest things not to miss in Mexico!

1. Take a Stroll Around Frida Kahlo's House

There are certain artists that everyone pays attention to whether they are a huge art buff or not, and Frida Kahlo is one of those artists. Famous for her self portraits, Frida Kahlo is possibly the most famous artist across all of Mexico. On a trip to Mexico City, you shouldn't skip the opportunity to visit the house where she lived and worked with her husband, Diego Rivera, and where she housed Trotsky when he sought asylum.

(Londres 247, Del Carmen, Coyoacán, 04100 Ciudad de México; www.museofridakahlo.org.mx)

2. Take a Cup of Coffee at the Iconic El Jarocho Café

There is some great coffee to be had around Mexico, but there is no coffee shop that is quite as iconic as El Joracho, which is located in the leafy Coyoacan neighbourhood of Mexico City. This is a no frills place – in fact, there is no seating, you have to sit on the street – but the atmosphere is great and the coffee is even better. El Jarocho has been open for over half a century so the owners really know what they are doing. When you need a pick-me-up, this is the place.

(Av. México 25-C, Coyoacán, Del Carmen, 04100 Ciudad de México; www.cafeeljarocho.com.mx)

3. Watch a Mayan Ball Game in Merida

If you thought that ball games were a recent phenomenon, you might want to think again, because there is evidence to show that ball games were popular even during the Mayan civilization. The most famous ball game from then is called pok-ta-pok, and involves keeping a ball above the ground just by using the hips and sometimes the forearms. If you let the ball drop, the consequences could be dire, because ritual sacrifice was often a part of the game. On Friday nights, the game is still played in Plaza de Independencia in Merida - fortunately without any sacrifice.

4. Indulge a Late Night Sweet Tooth at a 24 Hour Churreria

If you haven't ever eaten a churro, you truly haven't lived. The churro is essentially the Mexican version of a doughnut. It is piped out into hot fat so the shape is a long cylinder, and then it is covered in sugar. You'll be able to find this deliciousness all over the country, but if you happen to be in Mexico City, do not bypass El Moro, a 24 hour churro joint that has been keeping bellies full since 1935. Dunked into a creamy hot chocolate, there is no better late night treat.

(Eje Central Lázaro Cárdenas 42, Cuauhtémoc, Centro, 06000 Ciudad de México; www.elmoro.mx)

5. Get Down With Ancient History at the National Anthropology Museum

Mexico City is a city for museum buffs. In fact, the capital has more museums than any other city in the world! The diamond in the crown of Mexico City's impressive museum scene is undoubtedly the National Anthropology Museum in Chapultepec park. It is the largest and most visited museum in all of Mexico, and once inside you can find the most spectacular artefacts from Mexico's pre-hispanic history. Notable items include an Olmec wrestler statue dating to 1200 BC and an ancient Pakal tomb.

(Av Paseo de la Reforma & Calzada Gandhi S/N, Chapultepec Polanco, Miguel Hidalgo, 11560 Ciudad de México; www.mna.inah.gob.mx/index.html)

6. Try 7 Types of Mole in Oaxaca

Oaxaca, a state in south central Mexico, is unofficially the food capital of Mexico. Peruse the streets of Oaxaca City and you will soon understand why. There are many traditional dishes from Oaxaca but the one that is probably the most famous is mole. You could think of mole as a kind of Mexican curry sauce, and there are seven type. For something very robust, the black mole contains chocolate and smoked chillies, and for something fresher, the green mole contains the zingy tastes of lime and cilantro.

7. Descend Into the Cave of Swallows

Looking for an adventure like no other? You might be interested in The Cave of Swallows, which is a pit cave located in the state of San Luis Potosi. The cave is a huge, with a 370 metre drop that goes straight down. It is an extremely popular cave for extreme sports, and particularly with BASE jumpers who parachute into the cave for an adventure that will get your heart beat racing.

(Carretera a Tamapatz, Union de Guadalupe Tamapatz, 79760 Aquismon, SLP)

8. Go Whale Watching in Sayulita

The joys of Mexico are not limited to Margarita cocktails and tacos. It's actually a country of immense natural beauty, and if you make it to the beach town of Sayulita in Nayarit, you can go whale watching from November to April. Tour companies can take you right out on to the Mexican waters where you can see humpback whales frolicking in their natural habitat. Beats another day tanning on the beach, right?

9. Learn All about the Mummies of Guanajuato

Guanajuato is one of the most unique cities in all of Mexico, and it's certainly the only place where you will find mummies. The reason why there are mummies is because the local government placed a tax on families to bury bodies in the past. Many families could not pay the tax, and some of these bodies ended up being mummified. The museum has a collection of over a hundred mummies from this period, including the mummies of men, women, and children.

(Explanada del Panteón Municipal s/n, Centro, 36000 Guanajuato; www.momiasdeguanajuato.gob.mx/english)

10. Be Bowled Over by Puebla's Cathedral

If you are at all interested in religious architecture, you will have found your paradise in the city of Puebla, just a couple of hours south of Mexico City. Puebla Cathedral, the cathedral that you'll find slap bang in the centre of the main plaza is one of the most important churches in the whole country, and when you take in its beauty, you will have an understanding of why. So elaborate is the cathedral that it took more than 100 years to build, and contains 14 chapels inside.

(C. 16 de Septiembre s/n, Lerma Centro, Centro, 72000 Puebla)

11. Dive Into a Cenote in Tulum

Mexico is a country with incredible biodiversity and something that you might want to explore is the underground river system that can be found in Yucatan and Quintana Roo. A cenote is essentially a collapse of rock that exposes the water beneath, and you can find many of these in and around Tulum. The water is crystal clear, and you can dive into some of these cenotes for a magical experience. Dos Ojos is a great choice as it's one of the largest underground cave systems in the world.

12. Taste the Mexican Version of Pizza, a Tlayuda

There are certain Mexican foods that are world famous, and some that are hardly known at all. If you want to try a different kind of Mexican food, go for a tlyauda, which is a specialty of Oaxaca. A tlayuda is essentially a really large and crispy tostada with a bunch of toppings, and that's why it is often referred to as the Mexican version of pizza. There is normally a spread of beans, stringy cheese, salad items, and your choice of meat, whether that's a thin strip of beef steak of chorizo sausage.

13. Get Into the Festival Spirit at Bahidora

If you are somebody who loves to party at summer festivals, Bahidora is one of the best kept secrets on the festival circuit. This is a 24 hour party that is located just a few hours south of Mexico City, and it has attracted some of the coolest indie talent from around the world from bands like Matthew Dear to rappers as big as Snoop Dogg. The vibe is very relaxed and yet very fun, it happens in the most beautiful surroundings, and it takes place in May of each year *(http://bahidora.com)*

14. Chow Down on Ants Eggs

Do you consider yourself to be an adventurous person? If so, you might want to try a Mexican delicacy that might seem a little odd first of all: ant's eggs. That's right, ant's eggs or escamoles as they are called in Mexico are otherwise known as the Mexican caviar. Their taste is actually very inoffensive. They are soft and creamy and kind of taste like cottage cheese. Would you be brave enough?

15. Take in the View at Hierve El Agua

Journey for about an hour and a half outside of Oaxaca city and you will make it to one of the most stunning natural formations in Mexico. Hierve El Agua is a petrified waterfall that you have a stunning view of from an adjacent mountain. And on top of that mountain there are natural pools where you can take a refreshing dip and take in the view of the waterfall and the mountains surrounding you. Get there early and spend the whole day.

16. Cheer on a Luchador at a Lucha Libre Match

Looking for a fun Friday night to remember? Forget the local bar and take in a Lucha Libre match instead. Lucha Libre is essentially a form of staged Mexican wrestling, and it is hugely popular. The wrestlers wear elaborate costumes and colourful masks that cover their faces. Huge arenas will sell out every weekend with punters who want to see an exciting wrestling match. Mexico City, Tijuana, and Guadalajara are all cities with a strong lucha libre culture.

17. Be Stunned by Cascading Waters at Agua Azul

Who doesn't love a day spent at a beautiful waterfall? You can find waterfalls all over the country, but none is more picturesque than Agua Azul in Chiapas. These are shallow cascades of the most stunningly blue water that drop one into the other. There are calm spots where you can make a little splash into the water, and you will be dazzled by the animal life all around you, from the fish swimming in the waterfall to the toucans in the jungle.

18. Celebrate Everything Oaxaqueno at the Guelaguetza Festival

Oaxaca is a state that is very indigenous, and people are extremely proud of their indigenous roots. The various indigenous groups and regions of Oaxaca all have different food, traditions, costumes, dances, and music, and the month long festival of Guelaguetza, which takes place every July, is a celebration of everything that is Oaxacan. During the month, you can enjoy a mole festival, a mezcal festival, and at the end of the month, a huge dance show in an enormous outdoor arena built specially for the festival.

19. Explore the Ancient Ruins of Teotihuacan

If you are in Mexico City and you want to learn about ancient Mexican civilizations not by hopping from museum to museum but by actually experiencing something, Teotihuacan, which lies just outside the city, makes for a fantastic day trip. Teotihuacan was in the fact the largest city in all of the Americas at its height in 200BC, housing 150,000 people. The ruins contain some of the largest ancient pyramids to be found anywhere in the world, and history buffs will love the experience.

(www.visitmexico.com/en/teotihuacan)

20. Tour the Lakes of Montebello

If you have downed just about as many margaritas as you can handle and you are looking for something that's a tad more peaceful, the Montebello lakes could be just the ticket. The lakes are actually old cenotes that with the erosion of the surrounding limestone have grown over time so they appear to be lakes. The lakes are famous for their bright colours, which occur because of the type of soil and the refraction of light. A few days boating and hiking around these lakes in Chiapas and you will feel fully restored.

21. Be Wowed by the Stunning Copper Canyon

The Copper Canyon is a jaw dropping set of six canyons in the state of Chihuahua, the overall size of which is actually larger than that of the Grand Canyon in Arizona. As you might imagine, this attraction is visually stunning, and this is one of few places where you can get a tourist train and view the surrounding landscapes from a train carriage. There is epic biodiversity all around, and the people living there are very traditional with cultures that go back for thousands of years.

22. Eat the Best Fish Tacos in Baja California

When in Mexico, you have to eat. And with so much coastline, one of the greatest things to eat is the fresh fish and seafood. Nothing quite beats a fish taco made with freshly pressed corn tortillas and fish caught straight from the ocean. Fish tacos are particularly popular in the state of Baja California. Just remember not to skip the hot salsa!

23. Chow Down on Corn Fungus

Being a vegetarian in Mexico is not impossible, but it isn't easy either, and if you're veggie you'll probably be eating a lot of cheese while on your trip. But something else that you can try is huitlacoche., This is actually a blue-purple coloured fungus that grows on corn. It sounds revolting, but it's been named the truffle of Mexico. The taste is earthy and isn't a million miles away from a mushroom taste. It's especially nice within a quesadilla.

24. Get Political at Trotsky's House

When Leon Trotsky, the Marxist revolutionary, was condemned to death in his home country of Russia, he was granted asylum in Mexico, and he actually lived with Diego Rivera and Frida Kahlo for a period of time in Mexico City. If you visit the Mexican capital, be sure to visit Trotsky's old house in the Coyoacan neighbourhood, which has now been transformed into a museum of his life in Mexico. Look out for bullet holes in the bedroom wall – the remains of a failed assassination attempt.

(Rio Churubusco 410, Coyoacán, Del Carmen, 04100 Ciudad de México; http://museocasadeleontrotsky.blogspot.com)

25. Celebrate Carnaval in Veracruz

Carnaval is not a celebration that you typically see in Mexico, and it's more associated with other Latin American countries such as Brazil. But the carnival spirit is alive and well every year in Veracruz. On the first night of the celebrations, things are publically burned in the central square in order to eliminate their bad spirit. From then on, it's party time. You'll hear the sounds of marimbas, guitars, and harps all over the city, and many people will be dressed up and dancing in colourful costumes. Why not be one of them?

26. Indulge Your Inner Bibliophile at Biblioteca Vasconcelos

You might not think that visiting a library sounds like a very exciting way to spend an afternoon, but if you are at all interested in the contemporary architecture of Mexico, this library is honestly something extra special. The incredible structure takes over a space of 38,000 square metres and cost an astounding $101 million to build. It is a wonderful place to take in an incredible feat of architecture, or to simply relax with a good book.

(Eje 1 Norte Mosqueta S/N, Cuauhtémoc, Buenavista, 06350 Ciudad de México; www.bibliotecavasconcelos.gob.mx)

27. Take it All Off on a Nude Beach in Oaxaca

The coast of the state of Oaxaca is somewhat neglected by people visiting Mexico in favour of the better known beaches in the Yucatan and in Baja California, but if it's beach time that you're after, do not neglect places like Huatulco, Mazunte, and Zipolite. Zipolite has something extra special about it because it contains one secluded nude beach. This is a coastal town where anything goes, so if you want to take it all off and get a full body tan, you will be more than welcome to do so.

28. Take the Train to Tequila

Don't lie, we know that you're headed to Mexico in order to sip on tequila day and night, and truth be told, that is not a terrible plan. But if you really want to get under the skin of tequila, you need to visit the birthplace of Mexico's most famous drink, which is also called Tequila! Once in Tequila, you can visit distilleries and sample a whole lot of the good stuff, but one of the most fun parts is the journey there, on one of the only trains in Mexico. As you journey, you'll see fields full of beautiful agaves.

(http://tequilaexpress.mx)

29. Discover the Incredible Handicrafts of Durango

Mexico has a history that extends back for thousands of years. That is most evident in the ruins located around the country, but you can also see incredible traditions in the handicrafts of the Mexican people, and especially in the state of Durango. The Gomez Palacio Market is a place in the centre where you can buy all kinds of handmade items, and something extra special is the jicara. A jicara is a bowl made from a dried out husk of a fruit, and it is hand painted with the most extraordinary patterns and colours.

30. Watch a Traditional Dance Show by the Ballet Folklorico

The traditional dances of Mexico are beyond beautiful. If you get a chance, you need to see the Ballet Folklorico de Mexico, which is a traditional Mexican dance ensemble based in Mexico City. The ensemble has more than fifty people, and the dances are often the traditional dances from pre-hispanic Mexico that date back for hundreds if not thousands of years. The troupe performs three times weekly at Bellas Artes in the centre if Mexico City, so there is no excuse not to see them perform.

(Violeta 31, Cuauhtemoc, Guerrero, 06300 Ciudad de México; www.balletfolkloricodemexico.com.mx)

31. Listen to Mariachi Music in Guadalajara

When you think of Mexican music, the first thing that you think of is the traditional Mariachi band. Mariachi is a type of music that originates from the 19th century in the city of Guadalajara. The band members always get very dressed up, and instruments include the trumpet, the guitar, the violin, and the accordion. In Guadalajara there is a whole plaza dedicated to mariachis, Plaza de los Mariachis. Head there on any night of the week to be serenaded by a live band.

32. Enjoy the Cervantino Arts Festival in Guanajuato

Mexico has an incredibly strong and diverse arts culture, and never is that more apparent than during the Cervantino arts festival, which takes place in the almost impossibly picturesque city of Guanajuato every October. The origins of the festival date to the mid 20th century when short plays were staged in the city's plazas, but now you can find all kinds of performances across multiple venues in the city. You can expect film screenings, literary talks, art exhibitions, operas, contemporary dance performances, a whole lot of street shows, and much more besides.

(www.festivalcervantino.gob.mx)

33. Fill Your Stomach With Tortas Ahogadas

Mexico is a huge country, and as you travel around you will find that the cuisine changes from place to place. Something very popular in the city of Guadalajara is called a Torta Ahogada, which translates as a drowned sandwich, and well, that's exactly what it is. A hearty grilled Mexican roll filled with some kind of meat is submerged in a spicy salsa sauce to mop up all of that bread.

34. Go Rug Shopping in Teotitlan Del Valle

When in Mexico, you are bound to be bowled over by all of the traditional crafts, and it's a lovely idea to take back something authentically Mexican for your home.

If you are impressed by Mexican textiles and rugs, head to Teotitlan del Valle outside of Oaxaca city, which has a weaving culture that dates back centuries. Everything is hand-made, hand dyed, and made with love and care. This means that the prices aren't rock bottom, but you are paying for something one-of-a-kind, and that will take pride of place in your home.

35. Visit a 19th Century Sweets Shop

If you have something of a sweet tooth, you are in luck because so do many Mexicans. You'll be able to find coconut filled limes, peanut candies, and Mexican fudge in many markets and shops, but there is one shop that really stands out from the crowd, and that is Dulceria de Celaya. This shop opened in Mexico City in 1874, and its withstood a great many earthquakes, and is still standing and serving up sweets today. The nougat covered almond is a particular highlight.

(Av. 5 de Mayo 39, Centro Histórico, Centro, 06000 Ciudad de México; http://ducleriadecelaya.com)

36. Catch a Movie at the Cineteca

It's more than possible to fill up your days in Mexico with incredible sightseeing and exciting adventures, but sometimes you just want to sit back and relax with a great movie. When that moment strikes, waste no time and head to the Cineteca in the Coyoacan neighbourhood of Mexico City. The building is amazing, the seats are comfortable, but best of all, the curation of the shows is outstanding. If you don't speak Spanish, there should be something in the programme in English for you to enjoy.

(Avenida México Coyoacán 389, Colonia Xoco, 03330 Ciudad de México; www.cinetecanacional.net)

37. Spend the Day in Picturesque Tlaquepaque

Guadalajara is the second largest city in Mexico, but if you find your time there a little overwhelming, you can simply hop on a bus to the outlying small town of Tlaquepaque. Tlaquepaque is especially great for a shopping outing. The streets are lined with shops that sell all kinds of arts and crafts, including ceramics, textiles, and jewellery. It's also a wonderful neighbourhood for an evening drink while listening to some mariachi music.

38. Eat the Best Tamales of Your Entire Life

There are some kinds of Mexican foods that you have probably heard of before, but haven't really appreciated just how delicious they are until you actually eat them inside Mexico. Tamales are one example. These soft cushions of masa get filled up with all kinds of ingredients, and one of the best places to try tamales is in Oaxaca, where you can find all the different kinds of mole (a complex, Mexican sauce) inside the tamal alongside pieces of chicken or pork. Tamales are typically sold at breakfast time, and often inside a bread roll for a really filling morning meal.

39. Relax Around Peaceful Lake Chapala

If you want just a little bit of respite from taco sellers selling their wares on the streets and the sound of street parades, why not try spending a few days relaxing around peaceful Lake Chapala in Jalisco? Lake Chapala is actually the largest freshwater lake in all of

Mexico, and because of its beautiful vistas and tranquil nature, it attracts many retirees from the States. Eat in one of the many surrounding restaurants for a lake view, or take a boat ride.

40. Visit the Majestic Chichen Itza

Mexico has an astounding history that extends back for thousands and thousands of years, long before the Spanish arrived. There are still signs of how people in the Maya civilization would have lived amongst the ruins that exist around the country, and perhaps the most famous of them all is stunning Chichen Itza in the Yucatan. Chichen Itza was one of the largest Mayan cities, and it dates way back to 900BC. To fully appreciate the various pyramids, temples, and other significant structures, it's best to use one of the park's guides to show you around.

(www.chichenitza.com)

41. Eat Some Tasty Treats at Mercado de San Juan

While there is absolutely no doubt that Mexico cooks up some of the finest grub in the world, there might be times when you are craving something other than a taco or a quesadilla. In which case, Mercado de San Juan in Mexico City is the place to go. If you are into the really exotic, you can pick up some strange meats such as iguana or rabbit, and if you simply want a delicious and filling bite, a baguette packed with cold cuts and a glass of red wine on the side should hit the spot.

(Calle de Ernesto Pugibet No. 21, Mexico City)

42. Take a Boat Trip Along the Canals of Xochimilco

Xochimilco is a region in the south of Mexico City that plays an extremely important role in the city's history. When early settlers arrived in Xochimilco, they were overwhelmed by the bogginess of the land, and so they built floating gardens that grew flowers, fruits, and vegetables on the water itself. The canals here are the remnants of those waterways, and you can take boat trips to see what life would have been like in 8th century Mexico City.

43. Visit Mexico's Only Royal Castle

Mexico has many historic buildings, but you probably don't associate the country with castles. Indeed, there aren't so many of them in Mexico, and, in fact, there is just one castle in Mexico City that can claim to be the only royal castle in North America. Chapultepec Castle, situated in the expansive Chapultepec park used to be the residence of Maximilian I during the second Mexican Empire. Nowadays it houses the country's National History Museum, and as it's built atop a hill, it's a fantastic spot for a view of the city. *(Bosque de Chapultepec I Secc, 11100 Ciudad de México; http://castillodechapultepec.inah.gob.mx)*

44. Visit an Archaeological Site in the Jungle

When in Mexico, you don't have to make a compromise between history and nature because you can find archaeological sites planted deep within the natural jungle. Take Calakmul in Campeche state, for example. Close to the Guatamela border, Calakmul was one of the most important cities in ancient Mayan times, with a population of 50,000. This site contains the largest known pyramid in the region, and it has some exceptionally well preserved murals.

45. Go Snorkelling in the Waters of Tulum

When you visit a beach town like Tulum, there is loads more to do than just sunning yourself on the white sand. If you want to have a real adventure, it can be a great idea to contact one of the many tour companies in the town and organise a snorkelling experience. The waters on this stretch of coast are exceptionally clear. As you swim, you will see colourful tropical fish, sea turtles, sting rays, and a selection of beautiful coral beneath you.

46. Try Tacos Arabes in Puebla

Puebla is a must visit city, with an assortment of stunning cathedrals and educational museums. But Puebla is sorely underrated as a foodie city as there is plenty to fill your stomach there as well. One of the highlights has to be Tacos Arabes, which literally translates as Arabic Tacos. These tacos were actually brought to the country by the Lebanese, and instead of the meat being piled on top of a traditional corn tortilla, they are placed on a fluffy flatbread made of wheat.

47. Tour the Botanical Gardens of Oaxaca

People come to Mexico for the beaches and for the food, but they often neglect the incredible countryside and plant life that you can find in the country. If you want some downtime in some beautiful gardens, the ethno-botanical gardens in Oaxaca are well worth exploring. What really sets apart these gardens from the crowd is that they weren't designed by gardeners but by painters, including the famous Francisco Toledo. Wild plants are used across the region for food, medicine, and crafts, so this is a very important place for the region.

(Reforma s/n, Centro, 68000 Oaxaca; www.bgci.org/garden.php?id=3161)

48. Chow Down on a Delicious Cemita

When in Puebla and you don't have time for a long and elaborate lunch, the best thing to do is to grab a cemita on the street. A cemita is essentially Puebla's answer to the humble sandwich. The bread is richer than other kinds of sandwich bread as it contains egg, and can be compared to brioche. The fillings inside are typically avocado, some kind of meat, cheese, white onions, a herb called papalo, and red salsa. Beats a BLT any day of the week!

49. Sip on Mezcal After Mezcal

It should come as no surprise that the Mexicans like to have a drink or two, but perhaps you have only tried tequila and Corona beers before. Well, if you haven't tried mezcal, you are in for a real treat. Tequila is actually a type of mezcal, but mezcal typically has a smokier taste then tequila because of the way that is aged. The centre of mezcal production is the state of the Oaxaca. There are mezcal distilleries that you can visit out in the country, and even more mezcalerias in the city where you can relax with a glass of the good stuff.

50. Buy Some Art in San Angel

Mexico is an artistic country, and Mexico City is an artistic city – but there is one part of the city where you can see art works lining all of the streets. Make your way to San Angel on any Saturday, and you will find a Saturday Bazaar and Art Fair. This is where local artists display their works in the parks and in the streets in the hopes that you will purchase something. Which, by the way, would not be a bad idea at all as many of the artists are very accomplished.

51. Take in the View on the Star of Puebla

If you are in Puebla and you are seeking out an incredible view, look no further than the Star of Puebla, which actually happens to be the tallest ferris wheel in all of North America, standing tall at a height of 260 feet. There are 54 climate controlled cabins that take its guests on a half an hour journey. At the top, you will be able to see many sights, including all of the city centre and its majestic cathedrals, as well as surrounding volcanoes and countryside.

(Osa Mayor 2520, Reserva Territorial Atlixcáyotl, Centros Comerciales Desarrollo Atlixcayotl, 72190 Puebla)

52. Get Back to Nature in the Sumidero Canyon

Just a few miles away from the capital of Chiapas, you can find one of the most astoundingly beautiful natural formations in all of Mexico: The Sumidero Canyon. This natural canyon is navigable by boat, and taking a two hour boat ride through the canyon is an extremely relaxing experience when and you'll be able to spot lots of local plant and animal life. If you want to take in the whole vista of the canyon, there are a few vantage points surrounding the canyon where you can take holiday photos to remember.

53. Have a Breakfast of Hot Chocolate and Bread in Oaxaca

One of the lovely things about going away is treating yourself to meals out. But if you want to try a more traditional breakfast and save some money at the same time, head to Oaxaca, where the most traditional breakfast is a piping cup of hot chocolate and a fluffy piece of sweet bread. The chocolate of Oaxaca is really something to behold - sweet, and creamy, and rich. And when you dunk your bread into the chocolate you will have an instant feeling of comfort, and you'll be full until lunchtime.

54. Explore Ruins in the Jungle in Palenque

When visiting the spectacularly green state of Chiapas, be sure not to miss a trip to Palenque, which was one of the most important cities of the Mayan civilization, dating back to 200BC and reaching its peak in the 7th century. While the site is smaller than somewhere like Chichen Itza, Palenque has some of the most well preserved buildings and details in all of Mexico, with beautiful sculptures and bas-relief carvings. After the city's decline, it was absorbed back into the jungle, and it's fascinating to see how the natural world and the ruins of Palenque meet.

55. Take a Surfing Lesson in Puerto Escondido

Are you the kind of person who likes to get active on holiday instead of lazing beside the pool all day? If so, the coast of Oaxaca, and specifically Puerto Escondido might just be the place for you. It's in Puerto Escondido that you'll find some of the most impressive waves in Mexico, and keen surfers from all over the world descend on this small coastal city to take advantage of the incredible surfing conditions. And you don't need to be an expert to join in the fun as there are tonnes of surf shops along the coast that provide lessons.

56. Climb the Angel of Independence

The Angel of Independence, located in the heart of Mexico City, is one of the most iconic figures in the whole of the country. It was erected at the beginning of the 20th century as a way of paying tribute to the heroes who fought for Mexico's independence, and you can often see crowds around the monument on days of national celebration. It's also possible to climb the 200 steps to the top of the Angel where you'll have a spectacular view – just be warned that it's a steep climb and not for the faint hearted!

(Paseo de la Reforma y Eje 2 PTE, Juárez, Cuauhtémoc, Ciudad de México)

57. Get Gruesome for Day of the Dead

Mexicans sure do know how to party, but there is one Mexican festival that stands out from the crowd, Day of the Dead or Dia de los Muertos in Spanish. This festival takes place on November 1st and 2nd each year, and it's during this time that Mexicans believe that the dead return to the earth for a limited period of time. It might sound gruesome, but the festival is actually really joyful. Oaxaca is probably the best spot to celebrate, and you'll find parties in cemeteries, parades along the streets (with people painted as skeletons), and people will buy decorative sugar skulls as well.

58. Eat Gay Tacos in Guadalajara

Mexico is a gay friendly country, but the capital of gay city life in Mexico has to be Guadalajara, the capital of Jalisco state, and the second largest city in the country. While you're in Guadalajara, you can hop from gay bar to gay bar, gay club to gay club, and at the end of your experience, you can chow down on gay tacos. Yup, Guadalajara is the only place in the country that has a gay taco stand. You can find Tacos Gay on Called Prisciliano Sanchez.

(Calle Prisciliano Sánchez 391-A, Zona Centro, 44100 Guadalajara)

59. Go White Water Rafting on the Papigochi River

If you happen to be visiting the Copper Canyon in the northern state of Chihuahua, you can indulge a sense of adventure by taking an adrenaline pumping white water rafting trip on the Papigochi River, which is in the same region. The water volume of the river has been categorised as a level 3. This basically means that the river runs fast and strong, and you'll want to hire an accomplished guide for your thrill seeking experience. This might not be one for first timers on river rapids.

60. Have a Gay Ol' Time in Puerto Vallarta

LGBT visitors to Mexico will have absolutely no problem finding places to party and have a gay old time. Mexico City and Guadalajara in particular are very gay friendly. But if you fancy more of a beach destination, waste no time and head straight to Puerto Vallarta on the coast of Jalisco. The town is pretty much a gay ghetto on the beach, with plenty of gay bars, gay clubs, and even a gay beach. The most popular times to visit are during Semana Santa and their Gay Pride week at the end of May.

61. Visit the Beautiful Cascada de Tamul

If you make it to the state of San Luis Potosi, and you are an outdoorsy kind of person, be sure to make a trip to the breath taking Cascada de Tamul, which happens to be the highest waterfall in the state, and unofficially the most beautiful in all of the country. The best way to see the falls is to visit the town of La Morena and then take a one hour boat ride out on the crystal clear waters of the river. At the end of your journey, you will have a perfect view of the majestic waterfall cascading downwards.

62. Climb a Volcano Outside of Mexico City

Mexico City is the kind of place to visit if you love eating out at restaurants, consuming street food, and hopping from museum to museum, but if you are more of an active person, you can also climb up a volcano that sits just outside of the city. Iztaccihuatl is a dormant volcano that has a height of 17,000 feet. There are a few tour companies that can take you hiking up the mountain, and there are different routes for different abilities. If you ascend high enough, you might even encounter snow!

63. Try Out Sportfishing in Los Cabos

Are you the kind of person who likes to try out new and exciting activities when you go on holiday? If so, Los Cabos in Baja California will have lots for you to explore, not least a spot of sportfishing. There are many companies that would be happy to take you out on their very impressive vessels, when you'll have the chance to catch fish from the middle of the ocean, such as tuna, marlin, sharks, and dorado. It beats putting a rod into your local pond any day!

64. Eat Conchinita Pibil in the Yucatan

One of the surprising things about the Yucatan region in the south of Mexico is that although it's famous for its coast, seafood isn't one of the staple foods. In fact, the most famous regional dish from the Yucatan is called Conchinita Pibil. This is a kind of slow cooked pork that is traditionally cooked underground, and the dish dates right back to the Maya civilisation. Nowadays, the pork isn't normally cooked underground but is slow cooked in orange juice and a red seed called achiote on the stove. You can eat it on tacos, on tostadas, in tortas, or simply how it is!

65. Sip on Endless Margaritas

Yes, Mexico has exceptional ruins and lots of incredible museums, but every now and then, you just need a beach day when you sip on cocktails from dawn until dusk. Of course, the most famous Mexican cocktail of them all is the margarita, which combines tequila with triple sec and lime juice. It's a simple but beautiful thing that originates in the north of Mexico, and that can now be found at virtually every beach bar in Mexico. Cheers to that!

66. See the World's Largest Tree Trunk

Okay, you probably didn't fly all the way to Mexico to see a very big tree, but if you just so happen to be in the city of Oaxaca, it's well worth visiting the Tule tree. The diameter of the trunk is a staggering 38 feet, and it has been alive for 2000 years. When trying to take a photo of the tree, it's pretty much impossible to get all of it into the frame, so you may have to deal with a selfie that just contains some of the branches!
(2 de Abril, 8va Etapa IVO Fracc el Retiro, Santa María del Tule, Oaxaca)

67. Eat Tacos Al Pastor After a Drunken Night Out

Every country in the world has its own version of drunk food, and in Mexico that is most definitely tacos al pastor, which translates as shepherd's tacos. The star of the show here is pork meat that has been marinated in a range of spices, including achiote, which is a spice that gives the pork meat a deep red colour. The meat is sliced from a spit on to soft corn tortillas and served with chopped onion, cilantro, and slices of pineapple.

68. Discover the Caves of Juxtlahuaca

Juxtlahuaca is a cave and archaeological site located in the state of Guerrero. If you are adventurous, potholing down into the ace is quite the experience, and once you are there, you will be rewarded by the most magical of sights. Inside the caves of this region you can find ancient Olmec paintings that date right back to 1200BC, making these the oldest known paintings in all of the Americas. The paintings are very clear and portray leaders, hunters, jaguars, and feathered serpents.

69. Catch a Great Movie at Morelia Film Festival

If you want to know how Mexico measures up to other countries with regard to contemporary arts, the Morelia Film Festival is a great place to start. The festival is right at the centre of Mexico's burgeoning cinema scene, and in the past big film names such as Gael Garcia Bernal, Javier Bardem, Jennifer Lawrence and Gus Van Sant have taken part in the festival. It takes place every October, and you'll be able to catch international movies as well as the works of up and coming Mexican film-makers.

(http://moreliafilmfest.com/en)

70. Enjoy a Heaping Bowl of Pozole

Mexico does comfort food extremely well, and perhaps the most comforting of them all is pozole. This is the Mexican version of a pork stew, and it often uses underused cuts of the animal, including its knuckles and cheeks. The pork is served in a spicy broth, and you'll also find hominy, which is a kind of plumped up chewy corn inside the dish. Garnished with lettuce, sour cream, and sliced radishes, you'll be back for bowlful after bowlful.

71. Dance, Dance, Dance at the Fiesta de Santa Cecilia

While in Mexico, you'll probably want to experience a mariachi performance or two. But if you really want to amp up your mariachi experience, there is one day of the year where you can hear mariachi songs all over the country, and that's for the Fiesta de Santa Cecilia. Saint Cecilia is the patron saint of the mariachis, and on this day, all the mariachi bands come together to sing her a raucous birthday song. Garibaldi Square in Mexico City is a great place to experience the festivities.

72. Experience a Mock Battle in Zacatecas

Zacatecas is one of Mexico's charming colonial cities, but if you visit at the end of August, you'll get to see a whole different side to the city. This is because you'll encounter a festival called La Morisma. At La Morisma, you will encounter a spectacular mock battle that re-enacts the triumph of the Christians over the old Muslims in Spain. The two rival armies, comprising 10,000 people, will then parade through the streets in full costume while lots of music plays.

73. Try an Ancient Mexican Drink, Pulque

Pulque is a love it or hate it drink, but you won't know until you try it! This drink, which is made from agave (the same as tequila, but tastes nothing like it) actually has a long and illustrious history, as it was the drink consumed by high priests in the Maya civilisation. Nowadays, it is something that Mexican grandmothers make in the countryside and that trendy twenty-somethings drink in Mexico City. It's slightly milky, slightly tangy, and it's usually served in a kind of fruit flavour, like strawberry or mango. Our favourite place to drink pulque is at Los Insurgentes in Mexico City.

74. Have an Artsy Day at the Soumaya Museum

If you want to spend a day perusing the galleries of Mexico City, you are in luck because this is an arts city that can compete with any other around the world. One of the more recent additions to the city's visual arts scene is Soumaya Museum, whose new building opened in just 2014. The museum contains a staggering 66,000 works of art, with many pieces from Europe and the 15th to 20th centuries. Some of the

famous art works on display include works by Monet,
Renoir, Rubens and Rodin.

*(Boulevard Miguel de Cervantes Saavedra 303, Granada,
Miguel Hidalgo, 11529 Ciudad de México;
www.soumaya.com.mx)*

75. Dance Your Socks Off at the BPM Festival

Playa del Carmen is known as one of the best places to
party in Mexico, and it draws hordes of party people
every year. If you take your partying extra seriously,
you need to know about the BPM Festival, which
takes place every January. As the title would suggest,
it's a festival for lovers of bangin' dance music. And
this festival is huge! It takes place across 10 days, and
over 300 acts perform across that time! For a mix of
beach weather and insane parties, BPM Festival is the
one.

(http://thebpmfestival.com)

76. Pick Up Silver at Taxco

Looking for something really special to take home
with you that will always remind you of your trip? You

can't do much better than a trip to Taxco, which is only an hour or so away from Mexico City, and Mexico's capital of silver. Taxco became one of the most important parts of the Americas for the mining of silver and you can spot quaint jewellery shops on the streets of this small town even today. The designs are beautiful, and you know that when you are buying jewellery in Taxco, you are getting the real deal.

77. Drink a Traditional Glass of Tejate

Mexico is a country full of traditional food and drinks, and one drink that you might not have heard of before is tejate. Tejate is a traditional drink in the state of Oaxaca that dates back to pre-hispanic times and is still popular with the local population. It is made from a mix of toasted maize, fermented cacoa beans, toasted mamey seeds, and cacoa flowers. The result is something that is refreshing yet rich, and that is the perfect thirst quencher for a hot day in Mexico.

78. Take a Horse and Carriage Ride Around Merida

Merida is one of the most beautiful cities in Mexico, but it's criminally underrated in favour of the close by beach destinations like Tulum and Cancun. Colonial era Spanish buildings can be found in all colours around the city, as well as beautiful cathedrals and even some Mayan stone work. The best way to leisurely take in all the beauty of the city is via horse and carriage. Yes, it's kind of a touristy thing to do, but it can also be a whole lot of fun. It's especially pleasant in the evening when the city lights up.

79. Explore the Ruins of Monte Alban

There are ancient ruins all over Mexico, and one of the most underrated is certainly the ancient city of Monte Alban on the outskirts of Oaxaca city. Monte Alban was the capital of the ancient Zapotec civilization, and it dates back to around 500BC. The site is not too difficult to walk around (although there is no shade, so do bring a hat) and as you walk you will find majestic temples, ball courts, tombs, and much more.

80. Indulge in Yummy Marquesitas

Do you have something of a sweet tooth? If so, you'll be glad to know that you can indulge on virtually any street in the Yucatan with a local specialty that goes by the name of marquesitas. A marquesita can be thought of as a cross between a crepe and a wafer. It was born in the 1930s when one street vendor put cheese inside a wafer and then covered it in cajeta, which is a local kind of caramel sauce. You can still try this traditional flavour, or you can opt for fruit flavoured jams, Nutella, or chocolate.

81. See Wild Flamingos in Celestun

It's not often that you get to see a group of beautiful flamingo right in front of you, but that's exactly what could happen on a trip to Celestun. The Celestun Bisosphere Reserve is a place of extraordinary natural beauty, where you can find mangroves, with lagoons, cenotes, and vegetation. This is the perfect place for lots of spectacular wildlife to thrive, including egrets, pelicans, herons, and, of course, the swathes of pink flamingos that the reserve is famous for.

82. Snack on Grasshoppers

When in Mexico, you'll want to try all of the different kinds of new foods that come your way (yup, Mexican food extends far beyond tacos, as delicious as they may be), and something that you probably haven't tried before is a grasshopper, or a chapulin as it would be called in Mexico. These are particularly popular in the colonial city of Oaxaca. Head to the 20 de Noviembre market, and you'll see indigenous women carrying around baskets of chapulines on their heads, just waiting for you to sample them.

83. Enjoy a Spectacular View of Zacatecas From a Cable Car

Zacatecas is a criminally underrated city in Mexico, and for those who love old architecture and are entranced by the colonial cities of Mexico, Zacatecas really has to be a must visit. And the very best way to take in all of the beauty of the city is via the Teleferico, or cable car. There are not many of these in Mexico, so this is a really unique feature of the city. The ride will take you all the way to the top of a mountain called La Bufa, and at the top you can also visit the Museum of the Fall of the Zacatecas.

84. Have a Smooch in the Alley of the Kiss

Guanajuato is a spectacularly beautiful city. The city is built on hills and valleys, and because the houses are painted in all kinds of bright colours, it could easily be mistaken for an Italian hill town. It's a great idea to walk the streets and take in all the beauty, but one of these streets is not like the others. El Callejon del Beso, or The Alley of the Kiss, is where couples go for a smooch. A kiss on the third step of the alley is said to bring fifteen years of happiness.

(36000, Patrocinio 58, Zona Centro, Guanajuato)

85. Wander Through the Home of Diego Rivera

Diego Rivera might just be the most famous artist that has emerged from Mexico. He is most famous for his frescoes, and you should absolutely take the chance to see them in buildings such as Bellas Artes in Mexico City. But if you also want to understand the man behind the art, be sure to visit Rivera's childhood home in Guanajuato. On the ground floor, his family home is recreated with 19th century antiques, and the upper floors show some of his early works and preliminary sketches.

(Positos 47, Zona Centro, 36000 Guanajuato; http://cultura.guanajuato.gob.mx/museos/diego.php)

86. Brush Up Your Spanish Skills

If you travel to Mexico, you'll soon realise that having some Spanish language skills under your belt is extremely useful. And outside of the big cities, not just useful but necessary. If your Spanish isn't quite up to scratch, there is an abundance of schools where you can give yourself a crash course, even if you are starting at zero. Some of the most popular places for studying Spanish are San Miguel de Allende, Cuernavaca, and Oaxaca.

87. Eat in Mexico City's Oldest Restaurant

There's no shortage of opportunities to have a delicious meal in Mexico City, but for something extra special book a table at La Hosteria de Santo Domingo, which just happens to be the oldest restaurant in the city, dating back to 1860. Check out the online reviews for this restaurant and you'll soon realise that they please their customers as much today as they did when they first opened. If you aren't sure what to order, we can recommend the chile en nogada, which is a chilli pepper stuffed with ground meat and dried fruit, bathed in a walnut sauce.

(Calle Belisario Dominguez 70 y 72, Cuauhtemoc, Centro Histórico, 06010 Ciudad de México; http://hosteriasantodomingo.mx)

88. Peruse the Barro Negro of Oaxaca

Mexico is a country full of crafts that go back in time before the Spanish arrived, and one such craft is Barro Negro, or black pottery, which can be found in Oaxaca. The reason it's called this is, of course, because the pottery is a deep black colour, and often very shiny, making it stand out from any other form of ceramics around the world. The clay isn't actually coloured but achieves its black colour in the firing process. A piece of this pottery would make a wonderful gift to take home with you.

89. Party With Bands on the Beach at Tropico

Acapulco was once the place to be for a glamorous getaway. Although the glamour of Acapulco is somewhat faded now, there is still one big reason to visit this coastal city, and that's a bangin' festival called Tropico. It takes place every December, so it's a fantastic place to escape the winter blues wherever you may be, and have an epic party on the beach. The festival specialises in dance and electronic acts, so if you love to dance, and you love beach weather, this is the festival for you.

(www.tropicomx.com)

90. Drink at a 130 Year Old Cantina, La Jalisciense

When in Mexico, you'll want to learn how to drink just like a Mexican does, and what better place to do so than at a traditional cantina that is over 130 years old? La Jalisciense opened way back in 1875 in the south of

Mexico City. It's still going strong today, and as you might expect, it has an old fashioned and well worn feel. The beer here is always flowing and reasonably priced, and their tortas keep the customers coming back for more.

(Plaza de la Constitución No.6, Tlalpan, Centro, 14000 Ciudad de México)

91. Explore the Mask Museum in San Miguel de Allende

San Miguel de Allende, a small city in central Mexico, is certainly one of the most artsy and cultural places in the country. If you are gallery and museum hopping, one of the highlights is sure to be the Mask Museum. The museum is actually housed within a B&B called Casa de la Cuesta, and you will find an incredible collection of more than 500 masks on display, many of which are very old and have been used in traditional rituals and dances.

(Cuesta de San José 32, Azteca, 37729 San Miguel de Allende; www.maskmuseumsma.com)

92. Explore the Largest Pyramid in the World

If you were to imagine where the largest pyramid in the world might be located, your first thought probably wouldn't be that it's in Mexico. But you would be wrong, because it does actually exist in Cholula, a small city just outside of Puebla. The Great Pyramid of Cholula stands at 55 metres in height, and was an extremely important religious and mythical centre in pre-hispanic times. It dates right back to the 3rd century BC, and visitors today can enter the pyramid through a network of tunnels.

(Av. 8 Norte #2, Centro, 72760 San Andrés Cholula)

93. Tour the Wineries of Valle de Guadalupe

The most popular drinks in Mexico are definitely tequila, mezcal, and beer, but if you are a wine lover, fear not because Baja California is total wine country, and it's in this part of the country that you'll find a selection of vineyards. And although this is a place for "New World" wines, it was actually Jesuit priests that started making wine here in the 18th century. Take a taxi, drive from vineyard to vineyard, sample some wines, and eat in the vineyard restaurants for an unforgettable experience.

94. Buy Local Handicrafts in Queretaro

If you still need to do some souvenir shopping, forget the shops with branded mugs and t-shirts, and search out the real deal in the city of Queretaro. It's here that you'll find a very special shop called Manos Quereteras, which translates as Hands of Queretaro. This is a space where traditional craft makers from the region can display their wares and showcase their indigenous culture. The textiles are particularly beautiful. A selection of purses from Manos Quereteras would make wonderful gifts.

(Avenida Constituyentes 3 Ote, San Francisquito, 76058 Santiago de Querétaro; http://manosqueretanas.com)

95. Behold the Incredible Colours of Tlacotalpan

As you tour around Mexico, you will soon understand that this is one of the most colourful countries in the world, and perhaps the most colourful town in the country is Tlacotalpan, located in the state of Veracruz. Tlacotalpan is actually so beautiful that the whole town has been declared a UNESCO Heritage Site. As well as playing host to a selection of colourful houses, a river runs through it where there are quaint eateries where you can grab a bite with a view.

96. Strut the Thursday Night Art Walk in Los Cabos

If you want to explore some of the arts scene in Mexico but you don't want to hop from gallery to gallery by yourself, the Thursday night art walk in Los Cabos could be just the thing you are looking for. Every week from November to June, you are invited to stroll the streets of Los Cabos with a group of like-minded people, check out the independent galleries, and sip on a couple of glasses of wine in the galleries. *(www.artcabo.com/art-walk.html)*

97. Be Enchanted by the Magic Town of Alamos

The small town of Alamos in the state of Sonora is known as one of Mexico's Magic Towns, and it's with good reason. As soon as you enter the town, you feel as though you are no longer in the 21st century, but have been transported back to an old Mexico of conquistadors and Spanish romanticism. While in the town, take your time walking around, and if you want to do something more adventurous, you can go horseback riding in the surrounding countryside.

98. Explore the Street Art of Oaxaca

Yes, Mexico has an exceptional arts culture, but you only really see one side of the Mexican arts scene when you visit galleries and museums. The other side of Mexico's visual arts culture can be found on the streets. One of the cities with an extremely vibrant street art scene is Oaxaca because this is both an artistic and a political city. The local government doesn't view street art as a public nuisance either, and some artists are positively encouraged to cover the city walls with their murals and slogans. When you witness the artistry first hand, you'll understand why.

99. Explore a Living Coral Reef in Baja California

Baja California is a popular beach destination for tourists who make the short journey down from the United States, but although the distance is short, the landscapes and culture are totally different. Something extra special is the Cabo Pulmo, which happens to be the only living coral reef in the Sea of Cortez, and largest of them in all of north America. The reef is estimated to be 20,000 years old, and if you have the opportunity to dive or snorkel there, be sure to grab it with both hands.

(Calle Santa Maria de la Rivera S/N, Centro, 23570 La Ribera; http://cabopulmo.com)

100. Take Home Some Stunning Poblano Talevera

When in Puebla, and you feel like taking a break from sightseeing around the cathedrals and museums, it can be a great idea to treat yourself with a spot of shopping. Puebla is a spectacular place to buy beautiful ceramics, and there is a particular variety of decorative pottery in Puebla that is called Poblano Talevera. This type of pottery only comes from the city and surrounding towns, because it is reliant on the local clay, and a local production process that dates back to the 16th century. It is decorated very intricately with a blue colour, and the technique was originally something that came from the Moors in Spain, that was then brought to Mexico.

101. Live Island Life on Isla Mujeres

There are tonnes of beautiful beach towns in Mexico where you can unwind on a relaxing break, but somehow a beach town doesn't quite compare to a tropical island, and fortunately Mexico has some of those as well. Isla Mujeres is one of the most beautiful, and it's just a short boat ride from the popular destination of Cancun. This is a laid back place where the best thing to do is simply take in the island vibes, but if you feel like being more active, a spot of whale watching or scuba diving should keep you busy enough.

Before You Go...

Thanks so much for reading **101 Amazing Things to Do in Mexico**. We really hope that this helps to make your time in Mexico the most fun and memorable trip that it can be.

Have a great trip, and don't eat too many tacos!

Team 101 Amazing Things